3-

Johnny Sandlin

FRONT COVER PHOTO
The rain-washed bricks of Deadwood's lower Main Street reflect a
palette of colors against the backdrop of its many historic buildings.

BACK COVER PHOTO
Dawn breaks over the bronze 5/4 scale sculpture Tatanka—Story of the Bison,
located just north of Deadwood on Highway 85.

TITLE PAGE PHOTO
Downtown Deadwood glows at dusk.

For Stephanie, Evan & Emmy

Thanks to Mary Kopco, director of the Adams Museum & House for her help
with the project, and to George Milos and the Deadwood Chamber of Commerce
and Visitors Bureau for their unbridled enthusiasm in making
Deadwood one of the most happening places in the West!

PUBLISHED AND DISTRIBUTED BY

**Johnny Sundby**
P H O T O G R A P H Y

4780 Easy Street
Rapid City, SD 57702
(605) 343-5646
dakota@rap.midco.net
www.johnnysundby.com

ISBN 978-09747152-1-2

*Text by Johnny Sundby*
*Designed by Ross Johnson Design Co., Rapid City, SD (rjdesign@rushmore.com)*
*Edited by Jill Sundby Van Alstyne and Mark Van Alstyne*

# DEADWOOD
## TOWN OF LEGENDS

PHOTOGRAPHS BY
# JOHNNY SUNDBY

Guns spinning and standing all of seven feet tall, Deadwood local Big Dave Murra gets ready for an evening shoot out on Main Street.

From left to right, Doug Wahl, Hugh McGraw, Marcus Volimas as Wild Bill Hickok, Randy Christensen and Sunday Bob Wilson pose for a photo at the Deadwood facade, located near near lower Main Street, after acting out the murder of Wild Bill Hickok.

A pistolier takes aim on Deadwood's Main Street during a historical reenactment.

Trolley driver Chet Borsch of Galena ferries passengers through Deadwood late at night. Deadwood operates six trolleys and plans to add two more by 2006.

Since 1989, when gambling in Deadwood was legalized by South Dakota voters, gaming revenues have funded historic preservation. This money has financed the restoration of brick streets, sidewalk clocks, street lamps, and other improvements evident throughout Deadwood.

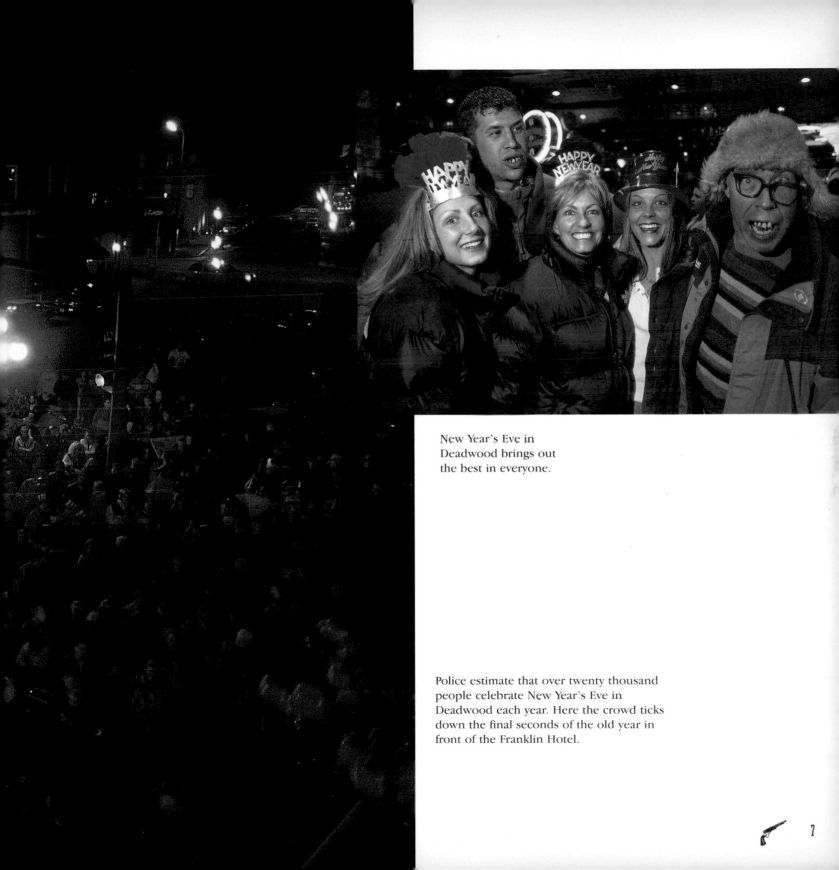

New Year's Eve in
Deadwood brings out
the best in everyone.

Police estimate that over twenty thousand
people celebrate New Year's Eve in
Deadwood each year. Here the crowd ticks
down the final seconds of the old year in
front of the Franklin Hotel.

Chet Ridenour of Rapid City gets a New Year's Eve kiss
from a friend at the Four Aces Casino.

From left, Jill Goldammer and Stephanie Myers of Mitchell enjoy friendship, slots and beer on a typically riotous New Year's Eve.

A cocktail waitress at actor Kevin Costner's Midnight Star takes a break. Deadwood's period costumes help keep the wild and colorful history of the town alive.

A young cowboy keeps an eye on events at the Days of '76 Rodeo.

A calf roper races after the prize at the Days of '76 Rodeo held in late July of every year.

Snow blankets Bear Butte, which lies at the mouth of Boulder Canyon. Bear Butte is a sacred place for Lakota and Cheyenne Indians who come for visions and to pray, and has long been a landmark for prairie travelers.

Tatanka—Story of the Bison lies north of Deadwood on Highway 85. The 5/4-scale, larger-than-life bronze sculpture is comprised of 14 bison being chased over a cliff by three mounted Lakota warriors. The work was commissioned by actor Kevin Costner and designed and created by Rapid City sculptor Peggy Detmers between 1994 and 2000. Tatanka—Story of the Bison can be visited between June 1 and October 15. For more information, go to www.storyofthebison.com.

Hiker Jennifer McGee enjoys the crystal waters of Cleopatra Creek at Devil's Bathtub between Spearfish Canyon and Deadwood near the abandoned Cleopatra Mine. The creek was formerly known as Squaw Creek, but the 2001 South Dakota Legislature changed the name of this and many other locations not deemed politically correct.

In addition to its abundant scenery, Spearfish Canyon near Deadwood boasts some terrific limestone rock climbing as demonstrated by Rapid City climber Matt Jackson on this 5.11 route at a climbing area known as "The Gully."

Elk Creek snakes through a spruce lined meadow near the Brownsville Road south of Deadwood after a heavy spring snow.

A Harley rider rolls through Deadwood during the Sturgis Motorcycle Rally, held in August each year.

Kool Deadwood Nites draws hundreds of
gleaming classic cars from all over the country.

Cars in Deadwood for Kool
Deadwood Nites take us for a
drive down Memory Lane.
Kool Deadwood Nites is held
every September.

Downtown Lead glows golden in the early morning sun. With a population of 8,392 in 1910, Lead was the second largest community in South Dakota.

A young woman talks on her cell phone at the same location where Seth Bullock opened a hardware store in 1876. Bullock later became Deadwood's first sheriff.

Charlie Utter Days bring out the best in the local population including Rose Mitchell-Speirs and Denise Neugebauer.

Some of the best ice climbing in the Black Hills is just outside of Deadwood in Spearfish Canyon. Here, Rapid City climbers Adam Pequette (left) and Matt Jackson practice maneuvers inside of Swallow Cave, high above scenic Highway 14A in Spearfish Canyon.

A father and son enjoy one another's company while angling for trout in the cool waters of Little Spearfish Creek just below Roughlock Falls in Spearfish Canyon.

Mary Ochse portrays Yellow Doll, an early Deadwood prostitute, in the Chinese New Year Parade. Yellow Doll was envied and loved by all but found her end in a vicious knife slaying by a jealous rival.

Chinese lion dancers from San Francisco bring in the Chinese New Year in front of Miss Kitty's on Deadwood's lower Main. The New Year is celebrated in late January or early February and is based on the lunar calendar. Vince and Joanne Coyle have reigned as Emperor and Empress and have organized the event each year since 1990.

An airborne racer crosses the finish line
in front of the Deer Mountain ski lodge.

Professional snowmobile racers
go head to head in front of ESPN
cameras every year at Deer
Mountain Ski Area in Lead.

Hundreds of classic cars line Main Street
and sparkle for passersby during Kool
Deadwood Nites, held every September.

Skier Bobby Sundby
makes new tracks
down Terry Peak after a
heavy March snowfall.
Terry Peak Ski Resort is
one of two ski areas in
the Black Hills.

Golden colors of fall
surround an early
1900's-era barn near
Terry Peak.

Joe Rovere performs an
aerial at Terry Peak Ski
Resort near Lead.

41

Kelsey Martin describes Deadwood's early mining
history at the Broken Boot Mine near Central City.

Wildflowers provide splashes of color near an abandoned barn south of Deadwood on the Brownsville Road.

The Grizzly Gulch Fire burned 11,589 acres and threatened the eastern and
southern edges of Deadwood in 2002. The town itself was named after dead
timber that prospectors found in the gulch now called Deadwood Gulch.

Water in Little Spearfish Creek tumbles over Roughlock Falls in Spearfish Canyon. The name Roughlock comes from a term meaning to lock wagon wheels while descending a steep grade.

An aerial view of downtown Lead shows how the Homestake gold mine's "Open Cut" has swallowed much of the town over the years, while still providing for the town's existence and survival.

At approximately 99 degrees Fahrenheit, 99 percent humidity, and more than a mile underground, miners in Homestake's North Drift drive rock bolts into the perimeter of the tunnel to distribute the downward pressure from above and protect against a possible cave-in. The mine operated continuously for 125 years until its closing in 2001.

Deadwood local Hugh McGraw portrays Canadian Seth Bullock, Deadwood's first sheriff, who started out selling hardware in this frontier town. McGraw also plays Lawyer Kuykendall in the Trial of Jack McCall.

Digby Reese poses for a photograph as Madam Dora Dufran. Digby and other locals bring historical information, drama, and excitement to the town, and are paid a small stipend from the city for their time and talents.

An "1858" .44 caliber Remington New Model Army revolver waits for a quick draw in a historic reenactment. This gun was one of the most powerful and well-built cap-and-ball percussion revolvers of its time. It is a six-shooter, firing round balls on top of black powder ignited with percussion caps. Made from 1863 until 1875, with a total production of 132,000, it was the last percussion revolver made by Remington and was one of the major handguns of the Civil War. After the war, many of these guns accompanied the soldiers to the "Old West." Most models are 13 inches long and weigh around two pounds.

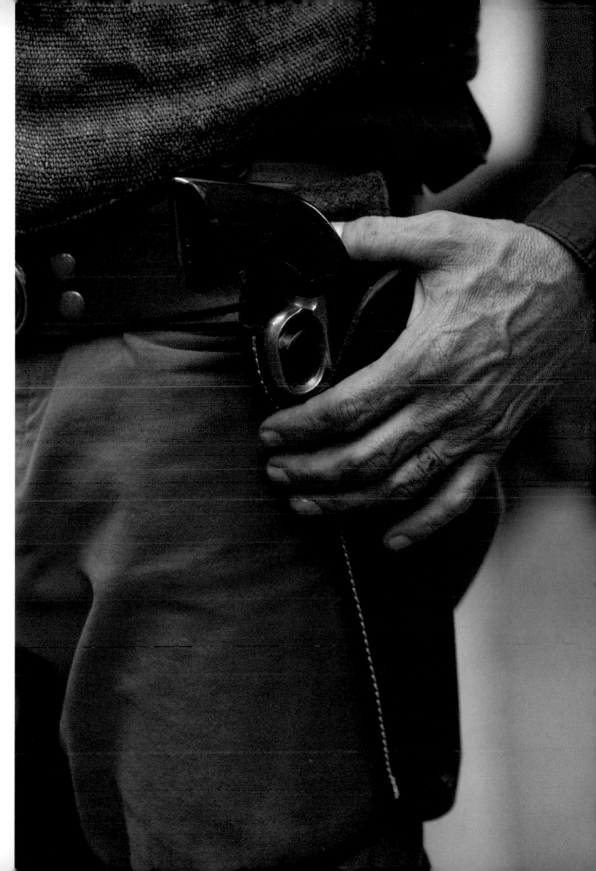

Engineer John Narem, welder Ken Haugen and engineer Bill "Robo" Robinson take a break 6,800 feet below the Earth's surface in the Homestake gold mine. Before its closing in December 2001, Homestake was the oldest, largest, and deepest mine in the Western Hemisphere. This mine, which is 8,000 feet deep, accounted for almost 10 percent of the total gold production in the United States since it opened in 1876. It produced nearly 40 million troy ounces of gold.

.E. Adams constructed the Adams Museum in 1930 as a memorial to his first wife, Alice, and his two deceased
aughters. In 1912, the Adams' eldest daughter, Lucile, died from typhoid fever. Then in June 1925, an infirmed
lice Adams was visiting their youngest daughter, Helen, who was pregnant with the Adams' first grandchild.
uffering from cancer, Alice succumbed to the disease. Several hours later, the grief-stricken Helen went into
remature labor and died in childbirth as did the granddaughter. Within 48 hours, W.E. Adams had lost his entire
mily, and thus this fitting memorial is in their honor.

The White Rocks high above Deadwood were visited by mule tours in the early 1900's. A short hike from Mount Moriah Cemetery to the rocks offers visitors a panoramic view of Deadwood.

Stephanie Sundby traverses through freshly fallen snow at Eagle Cliff, a 27-mile system of maintained cross country ski trails near Cheyenne Crossing, just west of Deadwood.

A dealer's hand nearly becomes a blur as she masterfully passes cards to blackjack players.

Denise Neugebauer enjoys a drink while trying her luck at
the slot machines at the Gold Dust.

Dryden, Caroline, and Bev
Hutter of Denver race
go-carts at Gulches of Fun.

Spearfish Creek tumbles lazily through birch, aspen, and spruce trees in scenic Spearfish Canyon.

A close-up look at Devils Tower National Monument just over the Wyoming border shows the giant columns created when igneous rock filled the core of an underground volcano.

Jimmy Ibbottsen and John McEuen of Nitty Gritty
Dirt Band fame entertain guests with "Mr. Bojangles"
at the 2000 Deadwood Jam.

Fabulous Thunderbirds,
Blues Traveler, Big Head
Todd and the Monsters,
Collective Soul and many
other big names have
headlined the Deadwood
Jam, held in the parking
lot of the Deadwood
Visitors Center
every September.

Along with those of Calamity Jane, Wild Bill, and Seth Bullock, Mount Moriah's graves tell many stories about Deadwood's population since the 1870's.

Seth Bullock and his wife lie high atop Mount Moriah Cemetery. Bullock arrived in Deadwood with his partner Sol Star in August 1876 and set up a hardware store on the corner of Main and Wall streets (the current site of the Bullock Hotel). When the turbulent town demanded law and order, Bullock was appointed Deadwood's first sheriff. His interests later spread to ranching, and he is credited with founding the nearby cattle town of Belle Fourche. Theodore Roosevelt met Bullock in 1884 and they became instant friends. During the Spanish-American War, Bullock volunteered as one of Roosevelt's "Rough Riders" and attained the rank of captain. When Roosevelt was elected president, Bullock organized a group of fifty cowboys to ride in President Roosevelt's inaugural parade.

Wild Bill Hickok's grave is a mandatory stop in
Mount Moriah Cemetary.  This bronze bust by
sculptor David Young was erected in 2002.

Photo by John A. Sundby

Photographer Johnny Sundby has spent years getting to know the Black Hills. He has an eye for its landscapes and for its interesting characters and their stories. With his friendliness and genuine interest in his subjects, he takes the time to understand people and places, and is able to capture their defining characteristics.

Johnny photographed for the *Rapid City* (South Dakota) *Journal*, the *Associated Press* (Pierre, S.D.), and the *Miles City* (Montana) *Star* between 1989 and 1997. Based in Rapid City, he has been self-employed since then, shooting portrait and editorial assignments in and around the Black Hills.

Johnny's work has appeared in many publications, including *Climbing, Consumer Reports, Family Circle, Field & Stream, Forbes, Golf Digest, House and Garden, Lawyers Weekly, the Los Angeles Times, National Enquirer, Parade, People, Runner's World, Time, USA Today, Western Horseman,* and the *Washington Post.* He and his photographs were featured in a July 2003 article of *American Cowboy* magazine. In 1995, he was named "Best Photographer in South Dakota" by *Eyes on You* magazine.

His first book, *In God's Country: Photographs of the Black Hills & Badlands,* (co-authored with his father, John A. Sundby), continues to be a regional best-seller, with more than 30,000 copies sold. He released his second book in 2004, *Wyoming's Big Horn Mountains, Like No Place on Earth*, which has been very popular with locals, and also with those who frequent the area.

Johnny is a graduate of Augustana College in Sioux Falls, South Dakota, where he received Bachelor of Arts degrees in English and business administration, and worked as a photographer for the college and also as newspaper editor. In his free time, he enjoys reading about history, performing with the Lonely Rangers band, and carpentry. But mostly, Johnny enjoys spending time in the outdoors with his wife, Stephanie, and their two children, Evan and Emmy.